REAL ESTATE INVESTING MADE EASY

ESSENTIAL TIPS FOR BEGINNERS

BY

Steven D. Patterson

TABLE OF CONTENTS

INTRODUCTION

In this book, we will simplify the real estate investing process and give you with the necessary knowledge, techniques, and resources to get started on your path to real estate success. Whether you're looking to buy rental properties, flip houses, or invest in commercial real estate, we'll teach you all you need to know to make sound decisions and maximize your profits.

WHY REAL ESTATE INVESTING?

Before we get into the mechanics of real estate investment, let's look at why real estate is such a popular asset class among investors of various backgrounds and skill levels.

One of the most tempting aspects of real estate investing is the possibility for long-term wealth creation. Historically, real estate has shown to be a stable investment vehicle, with properties often increasing in value with time. This implies that investors can increase the equity in their homes and potentially make significant capital profits when they sell.

Furthermore, real estate ownership provides the chance to produce passive income from rental properties. By owning rental properties and leasing them to tenants, investors may generate a consistent stream of rental income that can complement their current income or act as their principal source of cash flow.

Furthermore, real estate investment offers a number of tax benefits that can assist investors maximize earnings while minimizing tax responsibilities. Real estate provides several tax benefits, ranging from depreciation deductions to mortgage interest deductions, allowing investors to keep more of their hard-earned money in their pockets.

Finally, real estate investing provides diversification benefits, allowing investors to reduce risk and establish a well-balanced investment portfolio. Investors can minimize market volatility and enhance overall risk-adjusted returns by diversifying their investment holdings among asset classes such as stocks, bonds, and real estate.

WHAT YOU WILL LEARN

In the next pages, we'll cover a wide range of real estate investing themes, including:

- - Learning about the foundations of real estate investing, such as different types of investment properties, financing choices, and investment methods.

- - Setting investing goals and creating a tailored investment strategy that reflects your financial objectives, risk tolerance, and time horizon.

- -Finding successful investment properties in today's competitive market, includes methods for discovering discounted properties, performing due diligence, and negotiating advantageous acquisition conditions.

- • - finance your real estate ventures, includes advice on obtaining finance, raising your credit score, and increasing your borrowing capacity.

- • - Managing and maintaining your investment properties, including best practices in property management, tenant screening, and rental property upkeep.

- - Monitor your investments and alter your strategy when market circumstances change, including cash flow optimization, risk mitigation, and return maximization.

Throughout the book, we will present practical guidance, real-world examples, and actionable recommendations to help you confidently and successfully manage the problems and possibilities of real estate investment.

Real estate investment has the ability to revolutionize your financial destiny, opening up new avenues for wealth development and prosperity. Whether you want to diversify your investment portfolio, earn passive income, or attain financial independence, real estate investing may assist.

In the following chapters, we will teach you the information, tactics, and tools you need to succeed as a real estate investor. From understanding the fundamentals of real estate investment to finding profitable investment properties and managing your investment portfolio, this book will provide you with everything you need to start your real estate career.

together!

CHAPTER 1:

UNDERSTANDING REAL ESTATE INVESTMENT.

Real estate investment is a dynamic and multifaceted field that provides numerous opportunities for individuals looking to accumulate wealth, generate passive income, and achieve financial independence. In this comprehensive guide, we'll look at the fundamentals of real estate investing, such as its advantages, risks, and various investment strategies. Gaining a deeper understanding of real estate investment will enable you to make more informed decisions and maximize your returns in the real estate market.

WHAT IS REAL ESTATE INVESTMENT?

Real estate investment is fundamentally the purchase, ownership, and management of properties with the expectation of a return on investment. Unlike other asset classes like stocks or bonds, real estate gives investors tangible assets like land and buildings. These properties can increase in value over time, generate rental income, and provide a number of tax advantages.

ADVANTAGES OF REAL ESTATE INVESTING

Real estate investment provides numerous benefits to investors, making it an appealing option for those looking to increase their wealth and achieve their financial objectives. Some of the primary advantages of real estate investment include:

- **-Potential for long-term appreciation**: Real estate has historically proven to be a dependable investment, with properties typically increasing in value with time. Investors who hold onto their properties for an extended period of time may benefit from significant capital gains.

• - **Passive income generation**: One of the most appealing aspects of real estate investing is the ability to earn passive income from rental properties. By renting out their properties to tenants, investors may generate a consistent stream of rental income that can complement their current income or act as their principal source of cash flow.

- **-Tax advantages**: Real estate investment provides a number of tax breaks that can help investors maximize their earnings while minimizing their tax bills. These advantages might include deductions for mortgage interest, property taxes, depreciation, and other expenditures involved with owning and maintaining investment properties.

- **Portfolio diversification**: Real estate investing may act as a helpful diversification strategy for investors wishing to diversify their risk across several asset types. By adding real estate to their investing portfolio, investors can lower their exposure to market volatility and increase their total risk-adjusted returns.

TYPES OF REAL ESTATE INVESTMENTS

Real estate investing involves a wide range of property kinds and investment techniques, each with its own set of advantages and drawbacks. Some of the most prevalent forms of real estate investments include:

- - Residential real estate consists of single-family homes, condominiums, townhomes, and multi-family apartment complexes. Residential real estate investment is popular among investors who want to earn rental income or flip houses for a profit.

- - Commercial real estate consists of office buildings, retail centers, industrial warehouses, and mixed-use complexes. Commercial real estate investing has the potential for bigger profits, but it also involves more risks and complications.

- **-Rental properties**: These are properties that are rented out to tenants in exchange for monthly rental payments. Rental properties may give investors with a consistent stream of passive income while also offering possible tax benefits.

- - Fix-and-flip ventures entail buying troubled houses, fixing them, and reselling them for profit. Fix-and-flip projects may be profitable, but they require meticulous strategy, execution, and market research.

- -Real estate investment trusts (REITs): REITs are investment entities that enable investors to participate in a portfolio of real estate assets without actually owning the properties. REITs offer diversity, liquidity, and access to income-producing properties.

THE RISKS AND CHALLENGES OF REAL ESTATE INVESTMENT

While real estate investing has many advantages, it also has its share of dangers and obstacles. Some of the main risks and problems of real estate investment are:

- **Market variations:** Real estate markets are cyclical, with swings in supply and demand, interest rates, and economic conditions. Market downturns can cause losses in property values and rental revenue, reducing investors' profits.

- Vacancies and tenant turnover can have a substantial influence on investors' cash flow and profitability. High vacancy rates can lead to lost rental income and additional expenditures for property upkeep and marketing.

- **funding difficulties**: Obtaining funding for real estate investments may be difficult, particularly for inexperienced investors or those with less-than-perfect credit. Tighter lending criteria, higher interest rates, and more stringent qualifying requirements might make it harder for investors to obtain finance for their properties.

-Property management difficulties: Managing rental properties may be time-consuming and labor-intensive, as investors must deal with tenant concerns, maintenance requests, and property upkeep. Poor property management can result in higher expenditures, tenant unhappiness, and legal difficulties.

Understanding real estate investing is critical for anybody wishing to enter the real estate market and accumulate wealth through property ownership. Understanding the foundations of real estate investment, including its benefits, hazards, and numerous investment techniques, allows investors to make informed decisions and optimize their profits in the real estate market. In the following chapters, we'll go over each aspect of real estate investing in greater detail, offering practical advice, real-world examples, and actionable tips to help you succeed as a real estate investor.

CHAPTER 2:

SETTING YOUR INVESTMENT GOALS

Setting specific and attainable investment goals is essential for real estate investment success. By defining your goals and creating a road map for your investment journey, you can improve your chances of meeting your financial goals and building long-term wealth. In this chapter, we'll look at why it's important to set investment goals, what factors to consider when defining them, and how to create a personalized investment plan.

IMPORTANCE OF SETTING INVESTMENT GOALS

Before you get started in real estate investing, you must first define your investment goals and clarify what you hope to achieve. Setting clear and specific goals gives you a sense of direction and purpose, which guides your investment decisions and keeps you focused on what's most important to you.

IMPORTANT CONSIDERATIONS FOR DEFINING YOUR GOALS

When setting your investment goals, keep the following key considerations in mind:

1. **Financial objectives**: Think about your financial goals and what you hope to achieve through real estate investment. Do you want to generate passive income, build equity, increase capital appreciation, or diversify your investment portfolio?

2. **Risk tolerance**: Determine your risk tolerance and comfort level with various types of investments. Are you prepared to take on greater risk in exchange for

possibly larger profits, or do you prefer safer, more conservative investments?

3. **Time horizon**: Determine your investment time horizon and how long you plan to hold onto your investment properties. Are you looking for short-term gains through fix-and-flip projects, or are you in it for the long haul with buy-and-hold rental properties?

4. **Personal preferences**: Consider your personal preferences, interests, and lifestyle choices when setting your investment goals. Do you have a passion for real estate, or are you primarily

motivated by financial returns? Are you interested in a certain sort of property or investing strategy?

CREATING A PERSONALIZED INVESTMENT PLAN

Once you've defined your investment goals, it's time to create a personalized investment plan that aligns with your objectives and preferences. Here are some steps to help you establish a comprehensive investing plan:

1. **Define your goals**: Clearly explain your investing objectives, including your

intended financial results, risk tolerance, and time horizon.

2. **Assess your resources**: Take stock of your financial resources, including your savings, income, creditworthiness, and access to financing. Determine how much cash you have available to invest and what financing choices are accessible to you.

3. **Conduct market research**: Research the real estate market to identify potential investment opportunities that align with your goals and preferences. Explore different markets, property types, and

investment strategies to find the best fit for your investment plan.

4. **Create a strategy**: Using your goals and market research, devise a strategy for achieving your investment goals. Consider things like property selection, financing options, risk management strategies, and exit plans.

5. **Implement your plan**: Once you've created your investment strategy, it's time to put it into action. Start by identifying specific investment properties that meet your criteria and making offers on properties that align with your goals.

6. **Monitor and adjust**: Constantly monitor the performance of your investment portfolio and adjust your strategy as needed to reflect changing market conditions, new opportunities, and evolving financial goals.

Setting investing goals is the first step toward real estate investment success. By defining your goals, assessing your resources, and developing a personalized investment plan, you can lay the groundwork for a successful investment journey. In the chapters that follow, we'll go further into the many facets of real estate investing, giving you with the information, methods, and resources you need to reach your financial objectives and generate long-term wealth through real estate. So, are you ready to take the first step towards achieving your investment goals

CHAPTER 3

GETTING STARTED IN REAL ESTATE INVESTMENT

Starting out in real estate investment may be both thrilling and daunting, particularly for novices. With so many alternatives, techniques, and factors to consider, it's critical to approach the process with caution and preparation. In this chapter, we'll go over the essential stages for getting started in real estate investing, from expanding your knowledge base to picking the best investment plan for you.

EXPANDING YOUR KNOWLEDGE BASE

Before jumping into real estate investing, it is critical to get a good understanding of the market, investment methods, and potential risks and benefits. Here are some strategies to increase your knowledge base:

1. **Research**: Learn about market trends, property kinds, financing choices, and investing methods before making a real estate investment. There are several resources available to assist you learn more about the sector, such as books, articles, podcasts, and online courses.

2. **Education**: Consider taking real estate investment classes or seminars to broaden your knowledge and abilities. Many community colleges, universities, and online platforms provide courses in real estate finance, property management, and investment research.

3. **Networking**: Meet with seasoned real estate investors, industry professionals, and newcomers to learn from their experiences and obtain useful ideas. Joining local real estate investing groups, attending networking events, and participating in internet forums may all

help you develop a strong network of connections and mentors.

4. **Practical experience**: When it comes to learning about real estate investing, nothing matches firsthand experience. Consider beginning small by buying your own house or a rental property to obtain personal experience with property ownership and administration.

UNDERSTANDING MARKET DYNAMICS AND TRENDS.

Once you have a strong understanding of real estate investing, it is time to dig deeper into market dynamics and trends.

Understanding the elements that drive the real estate market can help you make more educated decisions and uncover successful investment possibilities. Here are some important industry characteristics and trends to consider:

1. **Supply and demand**: Supply and demand drive the real estate market, as they do in any other market. Population growth, job creation, and economic circumstances may all influence real estate demand, whereas zoning rules, building prices, and land availability can all have an impact on supply.

2. **Local market conditions**: Because real estate markets differ greatly from one region to the next, it is critical to conduct thorough study before investing. Consider population demographics, employment trends, rental vacancy rates, and median property prices to assess the market's health and stability.

3. **Economic indicators**: Monitor economic data such as GDP growth, unemployment rates, and interest rates, since they can all have an influence on the real estate market. Low unemployment and low interest rates, for example, tend to boost demand for real estate, but economic

downturns can cause property values and rental revenue to fall.

4. **Emerging trends**: Stay up to date on the latest real estate industry trends, such as technical breakthroughs, demographic shifts, and changes in customer preferences. These trends have the potential to provide new investment possibilities while also shaping the real estate industry's future.

FINDING THE RIGHT
INVESTMENT STRATEGY

With a good grasp of market dynamics and trends, it is time to select the best investing plan for you. There are several investing plans to select from, each with its own set of benefits and considerations. Here are some popular real estate investing options to consider:

1. **Buy and hold**: The buy-and-hold strategy is acquiring investment properties with the goal of holding them for a long time, usually to produce rental income and capital gain. This method is popular among investors looking to generate

passive income and accumulate long-term wealth.

2. **Fix and flip**: Fix-and-flip operations entail buying troubled homes, refurbishing them, and then reselling them for a profit. This approach has the potential to be profitable, but it takes careful preparation, execution, and market analysis to achieve success.

3. **Wholesale**: Wholesaling entails locating off-market agreements and selling the contracts to other investors for a price. To find profitable prospects, this method

involves good negotiation skills as well as a thorough awareness of the market.

4.Real-estate-crowdfunding:Crowdfunding platforms enable investors to combine their cash and invest in properties or real estate projects. This strategy enables access to a diverse portfolio of real estate investments without requiring significant capital or expertise.

ESTABLISHING A BUDGET AND FINANCIAL PLAN

Before making any investment decisions, you should create a budget and financial plan to guide your investment activities.

Here are some steps to help you make a budget and financial plan:

1. **Evaluate your financial situation**: Consider your current income, expenses, savings, and debt. Determine your available capital and financing options.

2. **Set investment objectives**: Determine your desired financial outcomes, risk tolerance, and time horizon. When defining goals, consider your age, income level, and financial experience.

3. **Establish your investment budget**: Based on your financial status and

investing goals, calculate how much money you can afford to put in.

Real Estate. When creating an investment budget, consider down payment requirements, closing fees, and continuing expenses.

4. **Create a comprehensive financial plan**: Outline your investment objectives, budget, financing options, and investment strategy. Consider working with a financial advisor or investment professional to develop a plan that is consistent with your goals and objectives.

IDENTIFYING INVESTMENT OPPORTUNITIES

With a budget and financial plan in place, it's time to look for investing possibilities that match your goals and tastes. Here are some tips for finding investment opportunities:

1. **Research the market**: Conduct market research to identify potential investment opportunities in your target market. Explore different neighborhoods, property types, and investment strategies to find the best fit for your investment plan.

2. **Network with industry professionals**: Connect with real estate agents, brokers, lenders, and other industry professionals to obtain access to off-market offers and useful knowledge about the local market.

3. **Attend real estate events**: Attend real estate conferences, seminars, and networking events to meet other investors and learn about new investment prospects. These events can also provide great education and networking opportunities.

4. **Use internet tools**: Take use of online resources such as real estate listing websites, investing forums, and

crowdfunding platforms to locate investment possibilities and interact with other investors.

EVALUATING INVESTMENT PROPERTIES

Once you've found prospective investment options, you must properly assess each property to verify it meets your investing goals and objectives. When considering investment properties, consider the following factors:

1. Location is one of the most important considerations when analyzing investment properties. Look for houses in desirable

communities with high rental demand, excellent schools, and easy access to services and transit.

2. Property condition: Assess the state of the property, including the age, layout, and condition of the structure and the status of main systems such as the roof, plumbing, and electrical. Factor in the cost of any essential repairs or improvements when evaluating your possible return on investment.

3. Estimate the property's rental income potential using comparable rental rates in the area. Consider market demand,

vacancy rates, and tenant preferences when calculating the property's potential rental income.

4. **Expenses**: Calculate the expenses associated with owning and operating the property, including property taxes, insurance, maintenance costs, and property management fees. Make sure to include in all expenditures when analyzing the possible return on investment.

5. **Financing options**: When analyzing investment properties, consider regular mortgages, hard money loans, and seller financing. Compare interest rates, periods,

and qualifying criteria to identify the most suitable financing choice for your investment strategy.

MAKE AN INFORMED DECISION

After examining possible investment properties, it's time to make an informed choice on which ones to pursue. Consider the property's location, condition, rental income possibilities, and expenditures while making your selection. Conduct due diligence, check all essential papers, and talk with trustworthy consultants to verify you're making the appropriate financial decision.

Getting into real estate investing may be a satisfying and successful undertaking, but it takes careful preparation, research, and implementation. Building a strong foundation of information, recognizing market dynamics and trends, choosing the correct investing strategy, and generating

Setting up a budget and financial plan, recognizing investing possibilities, appraising properties, and making educated decisions may all help you succeed as a real estate investor. In the next chapters, we'll go further into each facet of real estate investing, equipping you with the information, tactics, and tools you need to succeed in the market. So, are you prepared to take the first step in achieving your investment goals? Let us plunge in and discover the world of real estate investment together!

CHAPTER 4:

FINANCING YOUR INVESTMENTS

Securing finance is an important part of real estate investment because it allows investors to leverage their resources and buy properties they would not otherwise be able to afford. In this chapter, we'll look at the several financing alternatives accessible to real estate investors, such as typical mortgages, hard money loans, seller financing, and more. Understanding the various forms of financing and how they function allows investors to make educated decisions and optimize their investment potential.

UNDERSTANDING THE FINANCING OPTIONS

Investors have a variety of funding alternatives for their real estate projects. Each financing option has its own set of advantages, disadvantages, and qualifying criteria, so it's critical to thoroughly consider your alternatives and select the best financing approach for your investment objectives. Here are some popular funding alternatives for real estate investors:

1. **Traditional mortgages**: Traditional mortgages are one of the most popular financing alternatives for real estate investors. A classic mortgage involves the borrower (the investor) borrowing money from a lender (such as a bank or mortgage business) to buy a property. The borrower then pays back the loan over time, usually with interest, until it is paid off.

2. **Hard money loans**: Hard money loans are short-term, asset-based loans that are commonly utilized by real estate investors to fund fix-and-flip projects or other investment properties that do not qualify for standard financing. Hard money loans

are secured by the property itself, not the borrower's creditworthiness, making them an attractive choice for investors with less-than-perfect credit.

3. **Private money loans:** These are loans made by private persons or businesses rather than established financial institutions. These loans are frequently employed by real estate investors who want immediate funding or do not qualify for standard loans. Private money loans feature higher interest rates and costs than regular loans, but they provide investors more flexibility and speedier approval periods.

4. **Seller finance**: Seller financing, also known as owner financing or seller carryback financing, happens when the seller of a property lends money to the buyer (the investor) to ease the transaction. In seller financing agreements, the buyer makes periodic payments to the seller, generally with interest, until the debt is repaid. Seller financing can be a good choice for investors who do not qualify for standard finance or wish to negotiate better terms with the seller.

5. **Real estate investment trusts (REITs):** REITs are investment entities

that enable investors to engage in a diverse portfolio of real estate assets without actually owning the properties. REITs provide investors access to income-producing properties, capital appreciation possibilities, and portfolio diversification benefits.

6. **Crowdfunding**: Real estate crowdfunding platforms enable investors to combine their cash and invest in properties or real estate projects. Crowdfunding platforms often provide a wide range of investment options, from individual homes to large-scale real estate development projects. Crowdfunding

allows investors to have access to a diverse portfolio of real estate assets without requiring considerable funds or expertise.

CHOOSING THE APPROPRIATE FINANCING STRATEGY

When deciding on a financing approach for your real estate assets, you should examine your investment objectives, risk tolerance, creditworthiness, and available resources. Here are some suggestions for selecting the appropriate funding approach for your investing needs:

1. **Assess your financial situation**: Consider your savings, income, credit score, and availability to finance. Determine your accessible money and funding possibilities.

2. **Consider your investing objectives**: Think about your intended financial results, risk tolerance, and time horizon. Choose a financing option that is in line with your ambitions and will help you meet your investing objectives.

3. **Evaluate your creditworthiness**: Your creditworthiness is a major factor in determining your eligibility for traditional

financing alternatives like mortgages. Examine your credit report, correct any errors or anomalies, and take actions to enhance your credit score if needed.

4. **Investigate your alternatives**: Research several financing sources and compare interest rates, periods, and qualifying criteria. Consider speaking with a financial counselor or mortgage broker to discuss your alternatives and determine the best financing approach for your investment needs.

5. **Assess the costs and advantages**: Think about the costs and benefits of each

financing option, such as interest rates, fees, payback terms, and potential dangers. Choose a financing strategy that provides the best terms and is consistent with your investment objectives and risk tolerance.

NEGOTIATING FINANCE TERMS

Once you've decided on a financing strategy for your real estate investments, you must negotiate favorable terms with your lender or financing provider. Here are some tips to negotiate financing terms:

1. Shop around: Don't accept the first financing offer you receive. Shop around and compare offers from various lenders

or financing providers to ensure you get the best possible terms.

2. **Negotiate interest rates and fees**: Work with your lender or financing provider to lower your interest rate and reduce or eliminate any loan-related fees. A lower interest rate and fewer fees can help you save money over the course of the loan.

3. Look into prepayment options, such as early repayment penalties or prepayment discounts. Prepayment options allow you to have more flexibility and control over your loan repayment schedule.

4. **Read the fine print**: Carefully review the loan agreement's terms and conditions, including any clauses, restrictions, or contingencies. Before signing the loan documents, make sure you understand all of the terms.

5. **Seek professional advice**: Consult with a real estate attorney or financial advisor to review your financing agreement and make an informed decision. A professional can help you understand the loan's legal and financial implications, as well as identify potential pitfalls or risks.

Securing financing is an important step in the real estate investment process because it allows investors to leverage their capital and buy properties that they would otherwise be unable to afford. Understanding the various financing options available, selecting the best financing strategy for your investment goals, and negotiating favorable terms with your lender or financing provider will allow you to maximize your investment opportunities and meet your financial goals in the real estate market. In the chapters that follow, we'll delve deeper into each aspect of real estate investment financing, providing you with the knowledge, strategies, and tools you need to succeed as a real estate investor.

CHAPTER 5.

FINDING PROFITABLE INVESTMENT PROPERTIES

Finding profitable investment properties is a crucial step in the real estate investment process. Whether you're a beginner investor looking to purchase your first property or an experienced investor seeking to expand your portfolio, identifying properties with strong income potential and growth prospects is essential for maximizing your returns and achieving your investment goals. In this chapter, we'll discuss the essential tactics and approaches for locating lucrative investment properties, including performing market research, setting investment criteria, harnessing technology, and networking with industry specialists.

CONDUCTING MARKET RESEARCH

Before delving into the real estate market, it's vital to undertake extensive market research to find regions with significant investment potential. Market research entails studying numerous aspects that might impact property values and rental revenue, such as supply and demand dynamics, economic indicators, population demographics, employment trends, and local attractions. Here are some steps to perform good market research:

1. **Identify target markets**: Determine the geographic locations or neighborhoods where you wish to invest based on criteria such as market trends, growth potential, affordability, and your investment objectives.

2. **Analyze market trends:** Research historical and current market patterns to learn how property values and rental revenue have grown over time. Look for patterns and trends that may suggest

regions of growth or decrease in the real estate market.

3. Assess economic indicators: Monitor economic indicators such as GDP growth, unemployment rates, job creation, and income levels to measure the general health and stability of the local economy. Strong economic fundamentals may drive demand for real estate and boost property values and rental revenue.

4. Evaluate supply and demand dynamics: Assess the balance between supply and demand in the local real estate market by assessing measures such as inventory levels, vacancy rates, days on market, and rental vacancy rates. A tight supply-demand balance might suggest strong demand for properties and potential rental revenue increases.

5. Consider population demographics: Analyze population demographics such as age, income, family size, and migration trends to determine the makeup of the local population and their housing requirements and preferences. Population growth and demographic changes can impact demand for real estate and rental homes.

IDENTIFYING INVESTMENT CRITERIA

Once you've completed market research and identified potential markets, it's crucial to outline your investment criteria to drive your property search. Investment criteria are precise factors and preferences that you use to assess possible investment properties and determine if they meet your investment goals and objectives. Below are some common investing parameters to consider:

1. Property type: Decide whether you want to invest in single-family homes, multi-family properties, condominiums, townhomes, or commercial properties. Consider market demand, rental income potential, and your experience and knowledge of managing various property types.

2. Location: Determine your ideal location requirements, such as neighborhood quality, school districts, closeness to attractions, transit alternatives, and crime rates. Look for places with high rental demand, low vacancy rates, and potential for long-term growth.

3. **Investment approach**: Select an investment strategy that is appropriate for your aims and preferences, such as purchase and keep, repair and flip, rental properties, or real estate development. Each investment strategy has its own set of requirements, risks, and potential rewards, so select one that corresponds to your investment goals and risk tolerance.

4. **Financial measures:** Create financial criteria and benchmarks for assessing possible investment properties, such as cap rate, cash-on-cash return, gross rent multiplier, and return on investment. Determine your desired financial criteria

based on market trends, investing objectives, and risk tolerance.

5. Budget and funding: Create a budget for your home search and decide on financing choices, such as down payment requirements, loan terms, and interest rates. When creating a budget and researching financing options, keep in mind your available capital, creditworthiness, and borrowing capacity.

LEVERAGING TECHNOLOGY

In today's digital era, technology is critical to the real estate investing process, allowing investors to access information, analyze data, and uncover investment possibilities faster and more effectively than ever before. Here are some ways you may use technology in your property hunt.

1. Use online listing systems like Zillow, Realtor.com, Trulia, Redfin, and MLS to find available homes, examine property listings, and learn about market trends and property valuations. These systems allow you to filter homes by location, price, size, and property type, making it easy to identify properties that match your investment needs.

2. Real estate investing software: Purchase real estate investment software or tools that can assist you in analyzing properties, evaluating financial data, and assessing investment prospects. These tools frequently contain features like property value calculators, cash flow analysis tools, investment property databases, and market research reports, which provide you with useful insights and data to help you make investment decisions.

3. Virtual tours and 3D imaging: Use virtual tours and 3D imaging technologies to explore properties remotely and gain an understanding of their layout, condition, and characteristics without having to visit them in person. Virtual tours enable you to examine homes from various angles and views, resulting in a more immersive and engaging viewing experience.

4. Mobile applications: Download mobile apps developed for real estate investors to browse property listings, assess offers, watch market trends, and manage your investment portfolio on the move. These applications generally offer features such as property search tools, mortgage calculators, investment analysis tools, and portfolio management capabilities, allowing you to stay connected.

CHAPTER 6:

NEGOTIATING AND MAKING OFFERS

Negotiating and making bids are key steps in the real estate investment process. Whether you're buying your first investment property or adding to your portfolio, learning the art of negotiating and making persuasive offers will help you land successful transactions and optimize your profits. In this chapter, we'll look at the most effective methods and approaches for negotiating with sellers, creating competitive offers, and navigating the offer acceptance process to improve your chances of success in the real estate market.

UNDERSTANDING THE NEGOTIATING PROCESS

Negotiating a real estate transaction entails a series of contacts and exchanges between the buyer and seller to achieve an agreement on the terms and circumstances of the sale. Negotiation is both an art and a science, involving strong communication skills, strategic thinking, and a deep grasp of market dynamics and seller incentives. Here are some important factors of the bargaining process to consider.

1. Establishing rapport with the seller might assist to foster a friendly and effective bargaining atmosphere. Take the time to listen to the seller's issues, grasp their goals, and find common ground to foster trust and rapport.

2. Research and gather information on the property, market trends, similar sales, and seller motivations before beginning negotiations. Understanding the seller's situation, timeframe, and motives will

allow you to adjust your offer and negotiating strategy to their requirements and goals.

3. **Setting clear objectives**: Before beginning discussions, define your objectives and priorities. Determine your intended goal, acceptable conditions, and negotiating limits to help you plan your negotiation approach and make decisions.

4. **Presenting a compelling offer**: Create a compelling offer that meets the seller's goals and ambitions while preserving your interests as a buyer. Consider pricing, conditions, contingencies, and closing

timeframe when building your offer to make it appealing to the seller.

5. Effective negotiating skills include active listening, probing questioning, and taking a collaborative and solution-oriented approach to talks. Concentrate on creating mutually beneficial solutions that satisfy the seller's problems while also serving your own interests.

6. **Handling objections:** Anticipate and respond to probable objections or concerns made by the seller during negotiations. Be prepared to present data, explanation, or

alternative ideas to counter concerns and keep the discussion on track.

7. **Finalizing the agreement**: Once the terms and circumstances of the sale have been agreed upon, the agreement should be documented in writing and signed by both parties. Work with your real estate agent or attorney to create a purchase agreement or contract that defines the sale conditions and protects your buyer's interests.

MAKE COMPETITIVE OFFERS

Making competitive offers is critical to effectively acquiring investment properties in a competitive market. In today's competitive real estate market, buyers frequently compete with many offers for the same property, making it critical to create compelling offers that stand out to sellers. Here are some strategies for creating competitive offers:

1. **Determine your offer strategy**: Before making an offer, consider the market circumstances, property valuation, and seller motives. Determine whether you want to make an aggressive offer to secure the property quickly, or a more conservative offer to negotiate from a position of strength.

2. Conduct a comparative market analysis (CMA) to evaluate the property's fair market value and pricing in relation to other properties in the region. Use the CMA to help you determine your offer price and ensure that it is competitive and realistic given current market circumstances.

3. Consider the seller's objectives and conditions while creating an offer. Tailor your offer to meet the seller's needs and objectives, such as a quick closing, flexibility on the closing date, or willingness to address repairs.

4. Make a strong initial offer that demonstrates your seriousness as a buyer and positions you competitively with other potential buyers. Consider providing a competitive purchase price, favorable terms, and a reasonable earnest money deposit to demonstrate your commitment to the transaction.

5. Include a handwritten letter with your offer to identify yourself to the seller, explain why you're interested in the property, and show your excitement about the potential to buy it. A heartfelt letter

can help you stand out to the seller and leave a good impression.

6. Be adaptable and responsive to the seller's feedback and requests throughout the negotiation process. Respond quickly to counteroffers, address any concerns or objections raised by the seller, and be open to negotiating and compromising to reach a mutually acceptable agreement.

7. Work with a competent real estate agent: Choose a knowledgeable real estate agent who has negotiated and made offers in your desired market. A knowledgeable agent can offer valuable advice, market insights, and negotiation assistance to help you craft competitive offers and successfully navigate the offer acceptance process.

HOW TO NAVIGATE THE OFFER ACCEPTANCE PROCESS

Once you've placed an offer, the seller will analyze it and decide whether to accept, reject, or counter it. To establish a mutually acceptable agreement, you must navigate the offer acceptance process with patience, communication, and negotiating skills. Here are some ways to navigate the offer acceptance process:

1. Be patient: Give the vendor time to review your proposal and respond. Avoid putting pressure on the seller or setting unrealistic deadlines, as these can backfire and jeopardise your chances of obtaining the property.

2. Maintain open contact: Maintain open communication with the seller or their agent throughout the offer acceptance process. Stay in touch with the seller to answer any questions, address any concerns, and provide any additional information or documentation they may request.

3. Consider counteroffers: Be prepared for the possibility of receiving counteroffers from the seller. Evaluate any counteroffers carefully and consider whether the proposed terms are acceptable or if further negotiation is warranted. Be prepared to negotiate and compromise to reach a mutually acceptable solution.

4. Review the deal: Review the purchase agreement or contract carefully before signing to confirm that all terms and conditions are true and comprehensive.

Pay great attention to essential aspects such as purchase price, finance contingencies, inspection contingencies, and closing timeframe to avoid any misunderstandings or problems later on.

5. Consult with professionals: Consider speaking with a real estate attorney or adviser to analyze the acquisition agreement or contract and give information on any legal or financial ramifications. An experienced expert can assist you understand your rights and duties as a buyer and safeguard your interests during the transaction.

6. Prepare for closing: Once your offer is accepted and the purchase agreement is completed, begin preparing for closing by completing any remaining due diligence, getting financing, and working with appropriate parties like as lenders, inspectors, and title firms. Stay organized and proactive to guarantee a smooth and successful closure.

Negotiating and making offers are critical abilities for real estate investors, allowing them to obtain successful agreements and maximise their returns. By knowing the negotiating process, making competitive offers, and navigating the offer acceptance process successfully, investors may boost their chances of success in the real estate market. In the chapters that follow, we'll go deeper into each part of the negotiation and offer-making process, giving you with the information, methods, and resources you need to negotiate and obtain successful investment properties. So, are you ready to improve your negotiation skills and make compelling offers in the real estate market?

CHAPTER 7

MANAGE AND MAINTAIN YOUR PROPERTIES

Managing and maintaining your properties is critical to your long-term success and profitability as a real estate investor. Property management entails a variety of jobs and responsibilities, including tenant interactions, property upkeep, financial management, and legal compliance. In this chapter, we'll look at the essential ideas and best practices for managing and preserving your properties so that you may optimize their value and meet your investment objectives.

TENANT RELATIONS

Building great relationships with your renters is key for effective property management. Good tenant relations may lead to reduced vacancy rates, improved tenant satisfaction, and increased retention rates, eventually adding to the overall performance of your investment properties. Here are some techniques for creating healthy tenant relations:

- **Clear Communication**: Maintain open and transparent communication with your renters, giving them with clear expectations, guidelines, and processes for renting and living in your homes. Respond swiftly to tenant queries, requests, and concerns to demonstrate your dedication to their happiness and well-being.

- Respect and Professionalism: Always treat your renters with respect and professionalism, addressing them courteously and professionally during all contacts. Respect their privacy, rights, and personal space, and avoid participating in discriminating or invasive conduct.

- Fair and Consistent procedures: Establish fair and consistent procedures for rent collection, maintenance requests, lease enforcement, and other elements of property management. Apply uniform and fair policies to all renters to avoid charges of favoritism or discrimination.

-Timely Maintenance and Repairs: Respond to maintenance concerns and repair requests quickly and efficiently to maintain your properties' safety, comfort, and habitability. Schedule frequent inspections and maintenance checks to identify and fix possible problems before they become major concerns.

- Tenant Amenities and Services: Offer amenities and services that improve the tenant experience and increase the value of your properties, such as onsite laundry, parking, landscaping, and community events or activities. Consider tenants' preferences and needs when implementing amenities and services to maximise utility and appeal.

- **Conflict Resolution**: Create effective conflict resolution strategies to address any disputes or conflicts that may arise between you and your tenants. Listen to renters' issues, seek mutually beneficial solutions, and remain professional and polite throughout the resolution process.

PROPERTY MAINTENANCE

Regular maintenance and upkeep are vital for protecting the condition, appearance, and value of your investment properties. A well-maintained property not only attracts and maintains renters but also decreases the danger of costly repairs and property damage. Here are some suggestions for good property maintenance:

- **Preventive Maintenance**: Implement a preventive maintenance program to proactively detect and fix maintenance concerns before they progress into more major problems. Schedule monthly inspections, maintenance checks, and seasonal upkeep to maintain your properties in top condition.

- **Routine Inspections**: Perform routine inspections on your properties to assess their condition, identify any maintenance concerns or safety threats, and maintain compliance with local building rules and laws. Document inspection results, prioritize maintenance chores, and take remedial action as necessary to remedy any issues.

- **Prompt Repairs**: Respond quickly and effectively to maintenance concerns and repair requests to minimize tenant inconvenience and avoid future property damage. Create a system for reporting and monitoring maintenance requests, and prioritize repairs according to urgency and severity.

- **Landscaping and Curb Appeal**: Keep your properties' landscaping and curb appeal in good condition to increase visual appeal and attract potential renters. Keep lawns, gardens, and outside spaces well-kept and clear of waste, and invest in seasonal landscaping additions to improve the property's overall appearance.

- **Property improvements and Renovations**: Think about investing in property improvements and renovations to update and improve the functioning, comfort, and appeal of your homes. Focus on high-impact enhancements like kitchen and bathroom renovations, flooring replacements, and energy-efficient upgrades that increase property value and appeal to renters.

-**Emergency readiness**: Create an emergency readiness plan to handle unforeseen occurrences such as natural disasters, fires, or other situations that may affect your property. Create processes for reacting to crises, communicating with renters, and cooperating with appropriate authorities to protect the safety and well-being of tenants and property.

FINANCIAL MANAGEMENT

Effective financial management is critical to the financial health and profitability of your investment properties. It entails budgeting, accounting, rent collecting, spending tracking, and financial analysis to ensure that your properties create positive cash flow and meet your investment goals. Here are some ideas for successful money management:

- **Budgeting and Planning:** Develop a thorough budget for each of your properties, covering projected revenue, costs, and capital expenditures. Consider items such as property taxes, insurance premiums, maintenance charges, utilities, and property management fees when building your budget. Monitor your budget on a regular basis and make adjustments as needed to keep your properties financially sustainable and lucrative.

- **Rent collecting**: Set up a systematic rent collecting mechanism to guarantee that renters pay their rent on time and consistently. To ensure positive cash flow and reduce delinquencies, clearly communicate rent due dates, payment options, and late fines to renters, and regularly enforce rent collection rules.

- Expense Tracking and Management: Maintain detailed records of revenue and spending for each of your properties, including all income sources, operating costs, and capital expenditures. Accounting or property management software may be used to expedite spending monitoring and administration, as well as to provide financial reports that give information about your property's performance.

- **Reserve money**: Set up reserve money or contingency reserves to meet any unforeseen costs, vacancies, or capital renovations that may emerge while you own your properties. Maintain appropriate reserves to mitigate financial risks and guarantee that you can handle any unexpected costs without affecting your financial stability or property ownership.

- **Tax Planning and Compliance**: Stay current on tax laws, regulations, and incentives affecting real estate investment and property ownership. Consult a tax expert or accountant to create a tax planning strategy that reduces your tax burden while increasing your tax benefits as a real estate investor. you prevent penalties or fines, make sure you comply with all tax duties, such as property taxes, income taxes, and reporting requirements.

LEGAL COMPLIANCE

Ensuring legal compliance is critical for safeguarding your investment properties and avoiding legal liabilities or conflicts. As a property owner, you are subject to a variety of laws, rules, and duties that control landlord-tenant interactions, fair housing policies, property upkeep, and health and safety requirements. Here are some important issues of legal compliance to consider:

- **Landlord-Tenant rules**: Learn about the rules and regulations governing landlord-tenant relationships in your area, such as rental agreements, lease terms, eviction procedures, and tenant rights and obligations. Make sure your lease agreements follow all applicable rules and regulations, and that they include clauses to safeguard your rights as a landlord.

- **Fair Housing Practices**: Understand and follow fair housing laws and regulations that prohibit discrimination based on race, color, religion, national origin, gender, family status, or handicap in housing transactions. Avoid discriminatory activities or policies that may violate fair housing laws and subject you to legal action or penalties.

-Property Maintenance and Safety Standards: Keep your properties in accordance with local building codes, health and safety rules, and property maintenance requirements. Address any code breaches, safety dangers, or health problems as soon as possible to guarantee the tenants' safety and compliance with relevant laws and regulations.

- **Tenant Privacy and Rights**: Respect tenant privacy and rights by following the rules and regulations that regulate entrance into rental premises, privacy rights, and eviction procedures. Give renters sufficient notice before entering their apartments for inspections, repairs, or other purposes, and respect their right to peaceful enjoyment of the property.

- **Documentation and recordkeeping:** Maintain Accurate and thorough records of rental agreements, lease paperwork, rental payments, maintenance requests, and tenant correspondence. Keep documents structured and easily available for reference and documentation, and keep them for the statutory duration necessary to meet legal and regulatory obligations.

Managing and maintaining your properties is critical to guaranteeing your long-term success and profitability as a real estate owner. You may safeguard and optimize the value and profits on your investment properties by encouraging healthy tenant relations, employing effective property maintenance methods, managing money responsibly, and maintaining legal compliance. In the following chapters, we'll go over each area of managing and maintaining your properties in greater detail, giving you the information, skills, and tactics you need to thrive in the ever-changing world of real estate investment. So, are you ready to elevate your property management skills and achieve greater success in real estate investing?

CHAPTER 8

MONITORING YOUR INVESTMENTS AND CHANGING YOUR STRATEGY

Monitoring your investments and adjusting your strategy are critical components of real estate investment success. In a dynamic and ever-changing market, it is critical to regularly evaluate the performance of your investment properties, identify areas for improvement, and adjust your strategy to maximize returns while mitigating risks. In this chapter, we'll look at how important it is to monitor your investments, what key performance indicators to look for, and how to adjust your investment strategy to meet your goals.

THE IMPORTANCE OF MONITORING YOUR INVESTMENTS

Monitoring your investments allows you to stay up to date on the performance of your properties, identify trends and patterns, and make informed decisions to improve your investment portfolio. Actively monitoring your investments allows you to:

1. Assess performance: Evaluate your investment properties' financial performance, including rental income, expenses, cash flow, and overall profit. Identify properties that are performing well and those that may be underperforming or facing difficulties.

2. Identify trends and patterns: Examine market trends, economic indicators, and local factors that could affect the value and performance of your properties. Identify emerging opportunities or risks by tracking changes in rental demand, vacancy rates, property values, and economic conditions.

3.   Identify   opportunities   for improvement: Look for ways to enhance or optimize your investment portfolio, such as boosting rental revenue, lowering expenditures,   enhancing   property management, or introducing value-added methods. Determine any inefficiencies or bottlenecks that may be impeding the performance of your properties and take remedial measures to fix them.

4. Identify and reduce risks related to your investment properties, such as market volatility,   tenant   turnover,   property damage, or regulatory changes. Use risk

management tactics to preserve your investment portfolio and reduce possible losses.

5. Make educated decisions: Use data-driven insights and research to guide your financial strategy. Evaluate investment possibilities, weigh possible risks and rewards, and make smart decisions to improve your portfolio and meet your investing goals.

KEY PERFORMANCE INDICATORS TO TRACK

Tracking key performance indicators (KPIs) is critical for assessing the health and performance of your investment properties. KPIs give useful information about numerous elements of your properties' financial and operational performance, allowing you to measure their overall health and find areas for improvement. Here are a few critical performance metrics to monitor:

1. Occupancy rate: The occupancy rate is the percentage of occupied units in your rental properties during a certain time period. A high occupancy rate shows strong demand for your buildings and consistent rental revenue, whereas a low occupancy rate may imply vacancies or tenant churn.

2. Rental income: Rental income is the total revenue earned by rent payments on all of your investment properties. Monitor rental income on a monthly or quarterly basis to examine general trends and discover any variations or abnormalities.

3. Cash flow: Cash flow is the net income created by your investment properties after accounting for operational costs, debt service, and other financial commitments. Positive cash flow shows that your properties generate more money than costs, however negative cash flow suggests financial difficulties or cash flow deficits.

4. Return on investment (ROI): ROI calculates the return created by your investment properties in relation to the initial investment or total property value. To calculate ROI, divide the net income or profit made by the property by the initial investment or property value and represent the result as a percentage. Monitor ROI to determine the profitability and performance of your properties over time.

5. Cap rate: The capitalization rate (cap rate) calculates the rate of return on an investment property by comparing its net operating income (NOI) to its purchase price or property value. The cap rate is computed by dividing the property's net operating income by its acquisition price or value and expressing the result as a percentage. Monitor the cap rate to determine the investment possibilities and relative worth of your properties in comparison to other investment options.

6. Maintenance and repair expenses: Keep track of the maintenance and repair expenditures for your investment properties so you may analyze their general condition and detect any maintenance concerns or repair needs. Monitor maintenance spending patterns over time and take proactive steps to solve any concerns or postponed maintenance that may emerge.

7. Tenant satisfaction and retention: Calculate tenant satisfaction and retention rates to evaluate the effectiveness of your property management and tenant relations initiatives. Monitor tenant comments, reviews, and survey answers to identify areas for improvement and put in place initiatives to increase tenant satisfaction and retention.

STRATEGIES TO ADJUST YOUR INVESTMENT STRATEGY

Adjusting your investment plan is required to adapt to changes in market circumstances, economic considerations, or investment objectives. Flexibility and adaptability are essential for managing the real estate market and attaining long-term financial success. Here are some techniques to change your investing strategy:

1. Evaluate market circumstances: Conduct regular assessments of market conditions, economic data, and industry developments to uncover opportunities or threats to your investment portfolio. Keep track of changes in rental demand, property valuations, interest rates, and regulatory laws that may impact your investing plan.

2. Rebalance your portfolio: Rebalance your investment portfolio on a regular basis to maximize risk and return in accordance with your investment objectives and risk tolerance. When rebalancing your portfolio, keep asset allocation, diversity, and investment performance in mind to ensure that it remains on track for your goals.

3. Be open to new investing possibilities and asset classes that may provide attractive returns or diversification advantages. Consider diversifying your investment portfolio to include multiple property kinds, regional regions, or investment techniques that are appropriate for your risk profile and objectives.

4. Optimize property performance: Develop ways to improve the performance of your investment properties and increase their value and profitability. Consider property renovations, value-added enhancements, rent hikes, expenditure savings, or operational efficiency as ways to improve property performance and investment returns.

5. Adjust financing strategies: Review your financing options and consider refinancing or restructuring current debt to take advantage of lower interest rates and conditions. Investigate financing options such as mortgage refinancing, loan modifications, or debt consolidation to improve your property's finance structure and lower borrowing expenses.

6. Regularly assess and change your investing goals, objectives, and timetables in response to changing market conditions, personal circumstances, or investment priorities. Be flexible and adaptive while developing and adjusting objectives to ensure that they stay relevant and attainable over time.

7. **Get expert advice**: Consult with seasoned real estate specialists, financial consultants, or investment experts for help and recommendations on changing your investing plan. Seek advice from industry experts who may offer useful viewpoints,

knowledge, and ideas to help you make educated decisions and meet your investing goals.

Monitoring your investments and adjusting your strategy are critical to long-term success and profitability as a real estate investor. You may improve the performance of your investment portfolio and meet your investment objectives by actively monitoring key performance indicators, analyzing market circumstances, and modifying your investment strategy as appropriate. In the following chapters, we'll go over each facet of monitoring your assets and revising your approach, giving you the information, skills, and tactics you need to thrive in the ever-changing world of real estate investing. So, are you ready to take your investment strategy to the next level and have more success in the real estate market?

CONCLUSION

To summarize, real estate investment provides enormous opportunities for wealth creation, financial security, and long-term prosperity. Throughout this book, we've looked at the essential ideas, techniques, and best practices for becoming a successful real estate investor, from learning the foundations to efficiently managing and maintaining your properties. By following the ideas and advice presented in this book, you may start your road to reaching your financial goals and developing a profitable real estate portfolio.

First and foremost, knowing the principles of real estate investment is vital for making educated decisions and optimizing profits. We've spoken about the several sorts of real estate investments, such as residential, commercial, and rental properties, as well as the aspects to consider when assessing investment prospects, such location, market circumstances, and property attributes. Gaining a good grasp of the basics will enable you to recognize attractive investment opportunities and make educated investment decisions that are consistent with your goals and objectives.

Once you've found investment prospects that fit your goals, developing a sound investing plan is critical to your success as a real estate investor. We've spoken about the necessity of identifying clear investing goals, determining your risk tolerance, and creating a strategic strategy for buying and managing properties. Whether you're looking for long-term appreciation, rental income, or property flipping, having a clear investing plan can help you stay focused, disciplined, and on track to meet your goals.

Effective property management is another critical component of real estate investing success. We've looked at the fundamentals and best practices for managing and maintaining your properties, such as tenant relations, property upkeep, financial management, and legal compliance. You may safeguard and optimize the value and profits on your investment properties by cultivating strong tenant relationships, taking preventative maintenance measures, managing money responsibly, and maintaining legal compliance.

Monitoring your assets and altering your strategy is vital for reacting to changing market conditions, economic considerations, or investment goals. We've highlighted the significance of periodically analyzing the performance of your properties, tracking key performance metrics, and making educated decisions to maximize your investment portfolio. By keeping educated, proactive, and adaptive, you may spot emerging possibilities, reduce risks, and alter your investing plan to reach your goals and objectives.